AF578879
Author Kiesha Wright

While the author has made every effort to ensure that the ideas,statistics, and information presented in this book are accurate to the best of her abilities, any implications direct, derived, or perceived, should only be used at the reader's discretion.

The author cannot be held responsible for any personal or commercial damage arising from communication, application, or misinterpretation of the information presented herein.

I want to thank the one above for helping me write this book.

I want to thank my dear ones who were there to support me when no one else was there and encouraged me to write my first children's book.

I also want to thank the spirit of my mom and dad who gave me the courage and strength to fulfill my dreams and create a Christmas book.

I chant and pray every day for a better world for us and our Children. I hope you enjoy this wonderful and beautiful Christmas book!

All her children were having such a good time in the snow outside playing and throwing snowballs, while up ahead, they saw Bigfoot Mama. Even though her feet were in the snow, you still could hear her Bigfoot sound.

One of the children whispered to the other kid in his ears: "Here comes Bigfoot Mama with her Bigfoot!" Bigfoot Mama yelled out, "Come on kids, time to go home, dinner is waiting". One of the kids shouted, "We are having such a good time, Bigfoot Mama!" "I don't care if it is the holiday kids or the Christmas season, so get your little self together and let's go home, Dinner is waiting for you, my little ones!" Bigfoot Mama Said.

As they all arrived home, Bigfoot Mama said "Coats and hats off everyone and take off your shoes, guys. I don't want any snow on the carpet, please." As they all proceed to the table. They are all seated to eat the wonderful food Bigfoot Mama had prepared: chicken, mashed potatoes, broccoli, peas, corn, and a big chocolate cake for dessert, along with a great big glass of Milk.

Forks, spoons, and plates rattle while they eat their food with a happy smile and voices singing "Yum Yum Yum", humming while they're eating. "I know the food is good, but no Yum Yum Yum at the table. Eat and be thankful, my children." Bigfoot Mama said.

One of the children spoke out at the table "Can we go into town and look for a beautiful Christmas tree?" "No," Bigfoot Mama replied. The smallest boy asked "Why?" with tears in his eyes. Bigfoot Mama said again "No, I don't believe in Christmas trees, now off to bed everyone!" One of the children angrily replied, "You are so mean and don't want us to have a happy Christmas". He ran upstairs followed by the rest of the children with tears in their eyes.

The next day Terry, his Brothers and Sisters and Bigfoot Mama witnessed other children with their parents happily buying Christmas trees, and smiling with joy on their faces. One of the children asked Bigfoot Mama why she doesn't like Christmas. Terry, the oldest Boy said, "She is making us unhappy, so let's make her unhappy too. We will talk about her Bigfoot and how big it is; it will make her unhappy Too." The children jumped into the car as they concluded how to hurt Bigfoot Mama for denying them Christmas joy.

So, they got in the car, still happy with a smile, and proceeded home. As they entered their home, Terry began to try to make Bigfoot Mama feel bad. One of his brothers grabbed his arm to stop him. "Let's not do this. We are a family and it is Christmas time" the little one said to Terry. "Don't you understand; she's trying to make us unhappy?" The little kid asked Terry "No she isn't, she was brought up that way and she didn't have a Christmas of her own that's why she's taking it out on our Christmas season so, we must try to do something to make her happy and make her see that Christmas is one of the most important days of the year and it brings joy to everyone across the world."

ABC
1234

As they reached home, Bigfoot Mama looked at all of them and said "Up the stairs you go, wash your hands and face and get ready for your bedtime. You will have an early morning to rise and lots of housework to do. Don't forget to say your prayers, good night my beautiful Ones".

"I'm so tired," Bigfoot said as she sat down in her rocking chair, gradually closed her eyes and fell asleep till the next morning.

In the morning, she called the children down to do housework, instructing the two girls to work in the kitchen. One to wash the dishes, the second girl to dry the dishes, and sweep the living room floor. The boys are to go out and feed the horses and milk the cows.

Wow! The children cleaned everywhere and left nothing undone.

There was a strange knock on the door as Bigfoot Mama wondered who it was. Surprisingly the visitor was Mr. Dolittle. He owned a store in town where customers come in to buy fruit, vegetables, sugar, milk and flowers. He asked Bigfoot Mama if her children would be interested in a Christmas job at his store. Bigfoot Mama replied "I don't know, let's ask them". She called them in the living room and asked them. "Hey little ones, Mr Doolittle have a Surprise for you". They all gathered around. Mr. Doolittle asked them if they would like a Christmas job in his store. Terry yelled out first: "yeah!" and all the kids jumped up and down and said "wow, now we can make money for our Christmas gifts!" yes yes the kids yelled. "Great," Mr. Doolittle said, "You will start first thing in the morning, how about That?" "Wow!" the kids replied, jumping up and down. "We can't wait to get started!" They rushed up to bed looking forward to having their job working at Mr. Doolittle's store.

The next morning, they jumped up out of Bed, brushed their teeth, washed their faces, combed their hair and ran down to eat breakfast in a rush and out the door they all lined up to get in Big Mama's old car and she drove the kids to work.

"We are here Kids nervous and ready." the children said, waving goodbye to Bigfoot Mama as they entered the store.

Terry works at the cash register, and the two girls stack bread and Canned foods while the other two little boys sweep the floor of the store. On their break time, at lunch time, they all gather in a Cozy place to eat lunch and to discuss Bigfoot Mama's problem about Christmas.

"This is the best time to discuss Bigfoot Mama's Christmas problem. What we can do to show her love and write a wish to Santa Claus "Yes" Everyone agreed.

"I will write to Santa Claus and ask him if he could come down with his reindeer to see Bigfoot Mama and give her the biggest presents of all and take her to the North Pole to see how wonderful Christmas is.

The little Brothers and sisters yelled "yes!" and agreed.

So the little boy wrote to Santa hoping and wishing his letter would reach Santa. The kids continued to work at the store for two weeks to make enough Christmas money to buy Christmas gifts and a Christmas tree with decorations, even though Bigfoot Mama didn't like the idea of them spending their money on Christmas, since she did not believe in it.

Terry said to the other kids, "This is our last day at work and it is Christmas eve. We have made enough money to buy our gifts and our Christmas tree." The Little Brothers said, "What if Bigfoot Mama doesn't want to have a Christmas tree?" "Let me handle this. Don't worry, once we get the tree in, decorate it, and put lights on it, there's nothing she would be able to do about it," Terry replied

Well, Bigfoot Mama did see the Christmas tree and all the decorations and lights lighting up like stars. She didn't tell anybody that it reminded her of home and how much it reminded her how much she wanted to celebrate Christmas with her family. She wasn't able to receive Christmas gifts as a child, but seeing the tree in front of her living Room now brought tears to roll down her cheeks.

Terry and the other kids stood by and watched Bigfoot Mama go into tears and felt so sorry for her. "Hold up everyone, we can't forget to pick up the gifts from the stores. We need to go shopping. Are you ready, everyone?"

"Yeah," the others replied. With tears in her eyes, Bigfoot Mama turned her back and walked away, off the Kids went.

Terry and all the other kids ran out the door to catch the bus before the store closed downtown. The girls went to the Jewelry shop to buy some little trinkets for their friends, while the boys went to the sports shop to see what they could find for their friends. They just wanted small gifts to give everyone.

The little one went to the sports shop as well, but his mind was on the gift for Bigfoot Mama and how to find the perfect sweater to give her in this wonderful season.

Each one of them asked each other what they bought and everyone replied "We got all we needed and little things we feel our friends would like" Terry asked the little one what was in his bag, he smiled and said a big sweater for Bigfoot Mama that spelled out Merry Christmas with her name on it.

Their shopping was done and complete, they were on their way back home, with people cheering merry Christmas to everyone with the smell of the season Snowflakes falling and people singing Christmas carols songs and lighted Christmas trees, on the way home. They saw so much joy and happiness. The little Brother wondered if Santa Claus got his letter about their Bigfoot Mama because he wants so badly for Bigfoot Mama to know and feel the meaning of Christmas like everyone else cheer around the world.

As they rushed home to put their gifts under the Christmas tree, they looked out the window while listening to many people and children singing Silent Night, and Jingle Bells

Everything they hope for now is set under the Christmas tree, the girls holding hands in tears while Jerry and his other Brothers, pray for Bigfoot Mama to believe in Christmas. I sure hope Santa got my letter. “Enough looking at that tree you call Christmas,” she stomped her Bigfoot and said “Off to bed everyone, you can open your little silly packages in the morning– off to bed Everyone”.

While everyone was sleeping, Bigfoot Mama slept too. Suddenly, she heard some noise in the living room. As she proceeded downstairs, she met a man in a red suit with a red cap, white beard, by the chimney with a big green bag hanging over his Chimney. "This can't be real," the Bigfoot Mama said. "Who is this man and how did he get down my chimney with her flashlight in her hands?" She shines on his face. "Who are you"?

she asked "I am Santa Claus and I got a letter from a little kid here that wants us to make their Bigfoot Mama happy," Santa replied.

"Who is Bigfoot Mama?" Santa asked.

"I'm Bigfoot Mama." "Well I'm here to take you to the North Pole." she looked at him and said "This is unbelievable; this is not real." "You better believe," Santa replied.

"Come with me," Santa Claus said, "We are going to the North Pole for your Christmas." She asked in amazement. Santa rushes her out the front door and puts her on his Sleigh and up in the air like magic.

They went in the sky towards the north pole. Bigfoot Mama was so excited and her eyes got big as she could not believe it. As she traveled in the sky and through the stars with Santa, beautiful reindeers they finally landed in the north pole and all the workers were there working, singing and dancing. She walked around with Santa Claus and he showed her how he makes all the toys for the children all over the world. "I hope you are happy and enjoying what you see here at North Pole Bigfoot Mama?" He asked. "I am so happy I never saw anything so beautiful." Bigfoot Mama said "What a Christmas gift for me."

"And now I do believe in a Christmas."

All of a sudden, she ended up in bed. She thought it was a dream. She was so excited, she ran downstairs and looked at the Christmas tree and looked at the chimney to find Santa but he was not there, "Oh what a wonderful dream!" she called the children down and yelled out "It's Christmas Day!" They were so surprised because they knew Bigfoot Mama was not a believer in Christmas.

The little one said, "Wow Santa answered my letter and I am so happy that Bigfoot Mama believes in Christmas!" All the children and Bigfoot Mama gathered around the Christmas tree, singing carols and opening their gifts, as Bigfoot Mama thought, well I am not going to get a gift, but I am happy anyway, I saw Santa and went to the North pole and that's good enough for me.

The little one said, "Bigfoot Mama you have a gift too," Terry jumped in and said "We all got you something!" and when she opened her gift, it was a big red sweater. With tears in her eyes, she replied "I'll cherish this all my life and wear it every Christmas,"

The little one got in the corner and said "Thank you Santa for answering my letter and letting Bigfoot Mama see the meaning of Christmas."

"Merry Christmas Bigfoot Mama!" everyone yelled. As they all gathered around the Christmas tree holding hands.

Bigfoot mama says Happy Holidays to you all and enjoy the wonderful season of Christmas.

About Kiesha Wright

Kiesha Wright hails from the Bay Area. She grew up in a religious home and was given music lessons as a child. At the age of 7, Kiesha would sneak under the kitchen table and played music from her mother's pots, and pans. Kiesha's Mom realized her potential and bought her a toy piano to practice on. The Pastor saw her playing on the toy piano and said, 'I am going to put that little girl on the organ in Church one day!' - and when the time came, he gave her the opportunity to play in the choir.

Kiesha graduated from San Francisco State University with a degree in Music and Dance and with encouragement from her Mom who has passed away but gave her the courage to follow her dreams. Kiesha managed to make a name for herself in the entertainment business - performing as a tribute actor - all over the world. She has also performed with Tina Turner.

She has performed with 'Legends in Concerts' which gave her the opportunity to travel to many countries including South Africa, Indonesia, Canada, Hong Kong, Tokyo, Netherland-Antilles and Aruba. You might also have seen her being interviewed on some TV-sitcoms such as Good Morning America, Good-Day Sacramento, ABC 10 News Sacramento, Atlanta news Channel 5, Atlanta Georgia TV News, News 7 Sacramento, KPIX San Francisco, The Jenny Jones TV Segment, KSNV News 3 and many more. You might have also seen her in the movie (Paradise Club) - with Eric Roberts (brother of Julia Roberts) as a dancer and many others.

Kiesha always wanted to write stories about helping children and always fantasized about making a fairyland book. This book is about a little girl and her dog, who come across characters who have no courage - and she tells them to follow her and believe in themselves to achieve their dreams. It is not an easy journey she says to her friends but believing is the first step to success. And when you read the book, you will understand that your little ones can do and be anything they want in their life, only if they believe and have courage.

So Kiesha now showcases her talent as an upcoming author to inspire children with an open heart for them to see that they are our future.

And always remember, God is Good ♥